MW00965917

watch it
cook

by Ivan Bulloch & Diane James
Introduction by Prue Leith
Photography Daniel Pangbourne
Illustrations Emily Hare

TWO CAN ™

PRINCETON ■ LONDON

Published in the United States and Canada by
Two-Can Publishing LLC
234 Nassau Street
Princeton, NJ 08542

www.two-canpublishing.com

©2000, 1999 Two-Can Publishing

For information on other Two-Can books and multimedia,
call 1-609-921-6700, fax 1-609-921-3349, or visit our web site at
http://www.two-canpublishing.com

Created by act-two

Art Director: Ivan Bulloch

Editor: Diane James

Cookery Consultant: Betsy Goodman-Smith

Production: Adam Wilde

With thanks to Daniel and Carrie for letting us use their kitchen

All rights reserved. No part of this publication may be reproduced,
stored in a retrieval system or transmitted in any form or by
any means electronic, mechanical, photocopying, recording or otherwise,
without written permission of the publisher.

'Two-Can' is a trademark of Two-Can Publishing.
Two-Can Publishing is a division of Zenith Entertainment plc,
43-45 Dorset Street, London W1H 4AB

Hardback ISBN 1-58728-510-X
Paperback ISBN 1-58728-511-8

Hardback 10 9 8 7 6 5 4 3 2 1 02 01 00
Paperback 10 9 8 7 6 5 4 3 2 1 02 01 00

Printed in Hong Kong by Wing King Tong

contents

watch it cook

Cooking is a great skill to have and it's a lot of fun. Not only can you feed yourself, but you can impress your friends and family, too. It's a great way to make friends!

You will never stop learning. There will always be someone with a new recipe to share, or a different way of doing things. When you go to a restaurant, ask if you can meet the chef. Make your own cook book with your favorite recipes. Find out what people eat in different countries.

Cooking encourages you to explore new things. Once you know the basic techniques, you can invent your own exciting dishes.

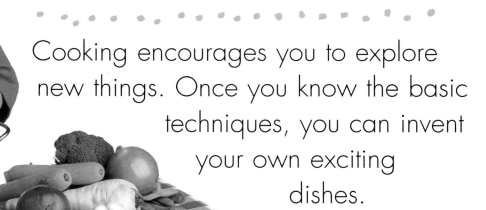

There is another side to cooking as well as having fun and experimenting. Once you become familiar with different ingredients, you can put them together to create a healthy, balanced diet.

Perhaps the best thing about cooking is sharing the results with other people. Sitting around a table with a bunch of people you like, enjoying a delicious meal that you have cooked is the best reward of all.

Have fun!

in the kitchen

Different jobs need different tools, and there are certainly lots of tools in a well-stocked kitchen! It's important to learn to use each tool properly and safely. Cooking is only dangerous when you are careless or try to do things too quickly. Be careful when you cut with knives and when you use heat. Make sure an adult is always on hand to help and advise.

What do I need? Before you start to cook, read through the recipe and gather together all the ingredients and equipment that you will need. Check how many people the recipe serves.

Saucepans
for cooking over heat

Mixing bowl
for mixing ingredients

Kitchen Safety

Know your knives
* Use a cutting board.
* Hold whatever you are cutting firmly but make sure your fingers are not near the knife.
* Always cut *away* from you.
* Put knives away when you have finished with them.

Beware of heat!
* Always use oven mitts when you are handling hot pans and dishes.
* Be careful of steam, which is extremely hot and can burn.
* Turn off heat when you have finished cooking.

Neat and tidy!
* Wash your hands before you handle food.
* Keep your hair well out of the way of food.
* Wipe kitchen surfaces carefully and mop up any spills as soon as they occur.

Wooden tools
for beating
and scraping

Electric beater
for beating large quantities

Whisk
for beating
small quantities

Measuring cup
for measuring
liquids

Measuring spoon
for measuring
liquids and solids

Heatproof dishes and pans
for using in the oven

Oven mitt
for holding
hot pans

Knives
for cutting
vegetables and meat

Gadget holder
for storing tools and utensils

Grater
for grating cheese,
onions, and apples

Colander
for draining
pasta and vegetables

7

what's cooking?

When you are planning a meal there's always a lot to think about. The first decision is *what* to cook! Always aim to include a balance of different kinds of food, whether you are preparing one dish, two, or even three. Think about color and texture, too. The most successful meals look good, smell good, and taste good. And they do you good at the same time!

Choose carefully! Eating a varied diet is a good way to stay fit and healthy. It's better to eat small meals during the day, rather than one huge one before you go to bed! As a chef, it helps to know how different foods keep you healthy in different ways. Then you can plan a meal that tastes delicious and is good for you, too! Look at the food groups on the next page and choose foods from each of them to make a balanced meal.

Pick-me-up!
A mid-morning drink of milk keeps the chef going. Milk contains fat, protein, vitamins, and minerals.

Looking good!
A well-balanced meal with something from each food group – *and* it looks colorful!

8

Body builders Proteins help your body grow and give you energy. Good sources of proteins are eggs, fish, meat, legumes, and nuts.

Fit and healthy Vitamins and minerals help prevent disease and keep your body strong. A really good source of both is found in fresh fruits and vegetables.

Energy Carbohydrates also give you energy. You'll find them in bread, cereals, potatoes, rice, and pasta.

More energy! Fats help your body store energy. You need to eat foods containing fat, but in small amounts. Foods with fats include butter, cheese, milk, and oil.

Chef's sandwich!
A perfect snack for a busy chef, packed with proteins, carbohydrates, vitamins, minerals and a little fat!

9

little nibbles

Here's an idea for when you and your friends are hungry, but don't feel like eating a big meal. Try a delicious, energizing snack instead. Snacks, or appetizers, are good for parties when there isn't room to sit around the table. They are sometimes called *finger food* because you don't need knives and forks.

Crunchy crudités Bite-size pieces of raw vegetables, such as carrots, peppers, and celery are delicious with a creamy dip. *Crudité* is French for *raw vegetables.*

Dip in Start with a base of thick, plain yogurt or mayonnaise. Add ketchup, grated onion, chopped herbs, curry powder, or mashed blue cheese.

Easy to eat Think about how people will be eating your snacks. If the snacks are for a party where people are standing up and do not have plates, make them small so they can be eaten in one or two bites.

Have fun experimenting with different ingredients and making up your own recipes.

Make it look good Preparing snacks gives you the opportunity to present a colorful display of food. When you shop, look out for interesting color combinations. Choose serving dishes to show off the different colors and shapes.

olive toasties & cheese bites

ingredients

Olive toasties   serves 4

1/4 of 8 oz. (227g) Cheddar cheese

1/2 onion

1 tablespoon mayonnaise

small jar of pitted black oliv

2 slices dark bread

Cheese bites   serves 4

small sprigs of parsley

1/4 of 8 oz. (227g) Cheddar cheese

1/4 of 8 oz. (227g) Monterey Jack cheese

1/2 of 8 oz. (227g) package cream cheese

2 tablespoons salad dressing (see page 12)

small crackers or squares of toast

tools to use

grater, mixing bowl, kitchen knife, cutting board, wooden spoon, oven mitts

Add chopped herbs as a finishing touch.

Cheese bites

Grate the Cheddar and Monterey Jack cheeses and place in a mixing bowl. Add the cream cheese and salad dressing. Mix together well. Spread on small crackers or squares of toast. Garnish with parsley sprigs.

Olive toasties

Turn the broiler on. Grate the cheese and onion and put them in a mixing bowl. Add the mayonnaise. Chop the olives and add to the bowl. Mix together. Toast the bread in a toaster. Spread the cheese and olive mix on the toast. Put the toast under the broiler for a few minutes until the topping is melted and slightly golden. Cool for a minute and cut into squares. Garnish with parsley sprigs.

salad bowl

Put washed lettuce between sheets of paper towel. Pat dry.

There are hundreds of recipes for salads, and, of course, you can make up your own! Favorite ingredients include lettuce, cucumber, and tomato – the fresher the better! Add some homemade dressing and toss everything together!

What goes in? Add cheese, cooked meat, or fish to a salad for a hearty main-course meal. Lettuce leaves with chopped herbs and a dressing make a perfect side salad to add taste and color to a fish or meat meal.

Salad dressing The best-known dressing is a mixture of oil and vinegar: 3 parts oil to 1 part vinegar, with a little salt and pepper. You can add small amounts of mustard, lemon juice, crushed garlic, and herbs. Whisk the ingredients together or shake them in a screw-top jar. Use enough dressing to coat the salad lightly.

Getting ready Wash and dry all the ingredients carefully. Cut vegetables into chunks and slices. Tear lettuce leaves. Make the dressing in advance and add it just before you are ready to serve.

Pre-cut vegetables Look for packages of pre-cut salad ingredients. This will save you washing the lettuce and give you more time to prepare the other ingredients.

A quick way to make dressing is to shake up the ingredients in a screw-top jar.

Mix or "toss" the salad with wooden spoons. Clean hands work well too!

tuna salad

ingredients serves 4

1/2 pound (250g) fresh green beans

1 yellow or orange bell pepper

1 small head of lettuce

6 oz. (170g) can tuna

1/2 cucumber

4 green onions

2 tomatoes

2 eggs

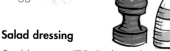

Salad dressing

5 tablespoons (75ml) olive oil

1 1/2 tablespoons (25ml) vinegar

salt and pepper

tools to use

two saucepans, vegetable knife, cutting board, colander, mixing bowl, can opener, fork, screw-top jar, salad servers, oven mitts

In the south of France, a salad made from tuna fish and olives is called Salade Niçoise. If you don't like tuna, try using small pieces of cooked chicken instead.

1 Put the eggs in a saucepan and cover with cold water by at least one inch. Heat water and eggs over high heat, just to boiling. Remove from haet, cover tightly, and let stand for 15 minutes. Fill one-fourth of a saucepan with water and bring to a boil. Cut the ends off the beans. Add the beans to the pan and return to a boil for 5 minutes. Drain and let cool.

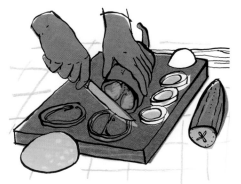

2 When the eggs are done, rinse them under cold water, peel the shells off, and cut into thick slices. Cut the pepper into slices and remove the seeds. Chop the green onions. Wash and dry the lettuce leaves and tear into bite-sized pieces. Wash the tomatoes and cut into quarters. Wash and slice the cucumber into 1/4-inch pieces. Put all the ingredients into a mixing bowl.

3 Open the can of tuna and drain. Use a fork to flake the tuna into the mixing bowl with the salad ingredients. Add the beans and eggs. Mix the salad dressing ingredients together. Pour the dressing over the salad and gently toss all the ingredients together.

soup of the day

There's nothing better than a bowl of hot soup to warm you up on a cold day, or chilled soup to cool things down when the sun is shining. Soup can be thick and creamy with chunks of meat, fish, or vegetables in it, or blended to make it smooth.

Start with stock Stock is the liquid that thins and flavors soup. You can make stock by simmering meat, fish, or vegetables in water for a couple of hours. Or you can buy a packet of bouillion cubes. Put one cube in a measuring cup, add the correct amount of boiling water, and stir until it dissolves.

A ladle helps to get the soup from the saucepan to a bowl or mug. Taste before serving to make sure the seasoning is right.

Simply smooth To make a smooth soup without lumps, pour the cooled mixture into an electric blender or food processor and blend until it is smooth. Or press it through a sieve with the back of a spoon.

14

pumpkin soup

ingredients serves 4

1 3-lb (1.5kg) pumpkin

1 onion

3 tablespoons (50g) butter

1 teaspoon ground nutmeg

1 teaspoon sugar

salt and pepper

4 cups (1 liter) stock

1 8-oz. (227g) carton of plain yogurt

handful of flat-leaved parsley

tools to use

baking tray, aluminium foil, vegetable knife, cutting board, large saucepan, wooden spoon, mixing bowl, measuring cup, electric blender, ladle, oven mitt

Serve your pumpkin soup with thick slices of crusty bread to make a filling meal.

1 Cover the baking tray with aluminium foil. Wash the pumpkin and put it on the tray. Put the tray and pumpkin in the oven. Set the oven to 350°F. Cook the pumpkin for one hour. Turn the heat off and leave the pumpkin in the oven to cool for at least another hour.

2 Peel the onion and chop into small pieces. Melt the butter in the pan over a low heat. Add the onion. Cook for about 10 minutes, stirring, until the onion is clear and soft. Stir in the nutmeg, sugar, salt, and pepper. Turn off the heat.

3 Cut the top off the cooled pumpkin. Scoop out the seeds and stringy bits with a spoon and throw them away. Take out the rest of the pumpkin in small spoonfuls, making sure not to include any outer skin. Put the pieces in a bowl and then add them into the saucepan with the onions. Return the pan to a low heat and stir for a few minutes until well mixed.

4 Make the stock in a measuring cup. Pour it into the pan. Stir well. Heat the soup to warm it, but don't let it boil. If it is too thick, add a little water. Let the soup cool slightly and put it in an electric blender or food processor. Blend until smooth. Ladle the soup into bowls. Add a spoonful of plain yogurt in the center of each bowl. Chop the parsley and sprinkle over.

vegetables

Different kinds of vegetables are available all year round, all over the world. There's a huge variety to choose from – so you'll never get bored. You can use vegetables to accompany meat and fish. Or, with the addition of a few extra ingredients, they make a delicious meal on their own.

Check it out! Buy the freshest vegetables you can. Look for bright colors and check to make sure they are firm and crisp. Don't buy anything that looks bruised or damaged.

Scrub and peel Wash vegetables to get rid of any soil or chemicals that may have been sprayed on. Peel or scrub vegetables such as potatoes and carrots. Take the outer skin off onions. Remove the coarse outer leaves from cabbage, cauliflower, and Brussels sprouts.

When you are slicing or chopping, use a sharp knife, hold the vegetable firmly, and keep your fingers out of the way.

Use a colander to drain boiled vegetables.

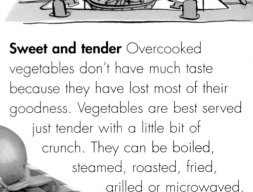

Sweet and tender Overcooked vegetables don't have much taste because they have lost most of their goodness. Vegetables are best served just tender with a little bit of crunch. They can be boiled, steamed, roasted, fried, grilled or microwaved.

vegetable pie

ingredients serves 4

2 small heads (150g) broccoli, stalks removed
1/4 medium-sized green cabbage
5 medium-sized mushrooms
1/2 teaspoon dried basil
2 medium-sized carrots
2 tablespoons (50g) butter
1/2 teaspoon caraway seeds
2/3 cup (150g) cottage cheese
salt and pepper
1/2 onion
1 egg
2/3 cup (150ml) sour cream
2/3 cup (150ml) plain yogurt

tools to use

paper towel, vegetable peeler,
vegetable knife, cutting board,
large saucepan, wooden spoon,
mixing bowl, small saucepan, whisk,
measuring cup, baking dish, oven mitt

This is a complete meal in itself, but you could serve it with rice to soak up the juices.

1 Heat the oven to 325°F. Wash the cabbage and broccoli. Peel the carrots and onion. Wipe the mushrooms with paper towel. Chop all the vegetables into very small pieces.

2 Melt half the butter in a saucepan over a low heat. Put all the vegetables in the pan, except the mushrooms. Stir for 5 minutes. Turn the heat off. Add the basil and caraway seeds.

3 Spoon the cottage cheese into a mixing bowl. Crack the egg into the bowl. Add a little salt and pepper. Whisk until the mixture is fairly smooth. Pour it over the vegetables and stir.

4 Melt the rest of the butter in a small pan. Add the mushrooms. Cook over a low heat until they have soaked up the butter. Turn the heat off.

5 Mix the sour cream and yogurt together in a jug. Lightly grease the baking dish and spoon in the vegetable mixture. Pour the sour cream and yogurt over the vegetables. Arrange the mushrooms on top. Put the baking dish in the oven. Bake for about 25 minutes until the yogurt and sour cream mixture has set. Use oven mitts to take the dish out of the oven.

good grains

Grains, such as rice, barley, wheat, and couscous, are packed full of protein. All grains come from plants. Rice is probably the best-known grain and is eaten by people everywhere. Most grains aren't expensive to buy and are useful to feed a lot of people. Just add a few of your own favorite ingredients.

All shapes and sizes You can buy whole grains, cracked grains, flaked grains, and ground grains. They are all hard and dry. Grains must be cooked to make them soft, plump, and tender. They are usually boiled or steamed.

Rice expands as it cooks. Use a large saucepan!

Put cooked rice into a bowl and separate the grains by fluffing them up with a fork.

Cooking rice Allow about 1/4 cup of rice for each person. Rinse rice in cold water to get rid of the starch. Measure the rice into a pan and add three times as much water. Bring to a boil. Lower the heat and put the lid on. Cook for 10 – 15 minutes. The rice absorbs all the water.

bulghur wheat

couscous

short grain rice

red rice

mixed wild and plain rice

18

COUSCOUS

ingredients *serves 4*

2/3 cup couscous

(if you buy pre-cooked couscous,
follow the instructions on the box)

2 stalks celery

6 green onions

2 tablespoons parsley

4 tablespoons lemon juice

4 tablespoons olive oil

4 tablespoons raisins

2 tablespoons pine nuts or unsalted peanuts

tools to use

mixing bowl, steamer or metal colander,
saucepan to fit colander or steamer, piece
of clean cheesecloth, vegetable knife,
cutting board, serving bowl, oven mitts

Couscous tastes as good cold as it does hot, so you can eat it in summer and winter.

1 Put the couscous in a mixing bowl and cover with warm water. If you don't have a steamer to cook the couscous in you can make your own. Line the colander with the cheesecloth. Fill the pan halfway with water. Put the colander on top.

2 Pour the water off the couscous. Put the drained couscous in the steamer. Bring the water to a boil over a high heat and then turn the heat down slightly. The steam goes through the colander and cooks the couscous, making it fluffy. Steam for about 10 minutes. Turn off the heat and let cool.

3 Finely chop the celery, green onions and parsley. Put them in a serving bowl with the lemon juice, olive oil, raisins, and nuts. Add the cooled couscous to the bowl. Mix everything together well. For a non-vegetarian couscous, you can add chopped cooked chicken or fish.

pasta

Pasta is a favorite food in Italy and just about everywhere else, too! There are hundreds of different pasta shapes which can be freshly made or dried. Pasta is ideal when you don't have much time because it cooks quickly. Add your favorite sauce and you will have a delicious meal in minutes.

Cooking Put plenty of water into a large pan. Add a tablespoon of oil and pinch of salt. Bring the water to a boil. Add the pasta. Stir to keep the pasta from sticking together. Bring the water back to a boil.

When you add pasta to boiling water, be careful of the hot steam. Lower long pieces in gently and allow them to soften a bit before stirring.

Al dente Cook the pasta until it is *al dente*. This is Italian for *to the tooth*. It means not too soft and not too hard. The best way to test pasta is to try a piece. Run it under cold water first. Start testing fresh pasta after cooking for 2 minutes, dried after 10 minutes.

A special pasta spoon with long prongs makes it easier to serve slippery spaghetti!

What to use The shape of pasta that you choose is up to you. But shells and bows hold thick sauces, while long pasta shapes are better served with thinner sauces. Dried pasta is handy because it keeps for a long time in the pantry. Fresh pasta cooks faster but does not keep as well. The best pasta is made from durum hard wheat.

Store dry pasta in air-tight jars.

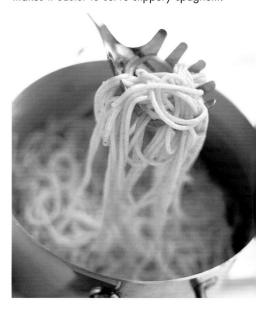

simple sauce

ingredients serves 4

1 garlic clove

1 onion

4 tablespoons olive oil

1 can (14.5 oz., or 400g) of diced
   tomatoes

1 tablespoon sugar

salt and pepper

1 teaspoon each dried basil, oregano

1/2 pound (300g) dried spaghetti

4 tablespoons grated Parmesan cheese

tools to use

knife, cutting board, medium-sized and
large saucepans, 2 wooden spoons,
can opener, colander, oven mitts

Sprinkle grated Parmesan cheese over before serving, or serve separately.

1 First make the sauce. Finely chop the garlic and onions. Put 2 tablespoons of oil into the medium-sized pan and heat it gently. Add the garlic and onions. Cook for about 8 minutes, stirring from time to time, until the onion and garlic are soft.

2 Open the can of tomatoes, being careful to avoid any sharp edges. Pour over the onion and garlic. Add the sugar, salt, pepper, and herbs. Continue cooking over low heat for about 20 minutes. Stir from time to time. Keep an eye on the sauce and begin cooking the pasta.

3 Add 1 tablespoon of the olive oil to a large saucepan of water and bring to a boil over high heat. Put the pasta carefully into the pan. Stir once or twice with a wooden spoon to separate the strands. Return the water to a full boil as quickly as possible and keep it boiling. Try a piece of pasta after about 10 minutes to see if it is ready.

4 When the pasta is cooked, drain it in a colander over the sink. Shake the colander to get rid of the water. Pour the pasta back into the large pan and add the tomato sauce. Stir to make sure the pasta is covered with sauce. Transfer to a serving dish and sprinkle with Parmesan.

fish and seafood

Many people think that cooking fish is difficult, but it couldn't be easier. Fish cooks in a matter of minutes, tastes delicious, and is full of protein.

Storing fish Keep fish in the refrigerator until you are ready to cook it. Make sure it is well covered with plastic kitchen wrap. Keep it away from other food.

Buying fish The fresher the fish you buy, the tastier it will be. But often you will have to make do with fish that has been frozen as soon as it is caught. If you shop in the supermarket, you'll find packages of different kinds of fish that have been trimmed, with the skin taken off and most of the bones removed. Large fish are cut into smaller pieces, and small or medium-sized fish are sold whole.

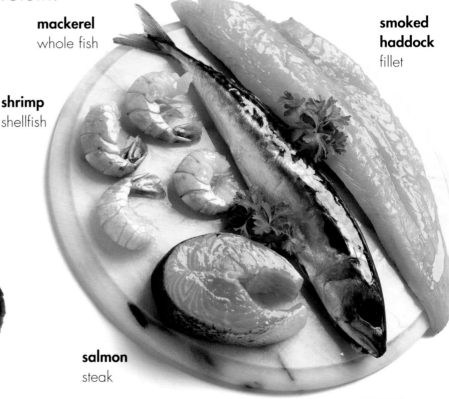

mackerel
whole fish

shrimp
shellfish

smoked haddock
fillet

salmon
steak

Cooking fish On the whole, fish cooks more quickly than meat. Thin fillets cook in a few minutes, while chunky steaks may take 5 – 10 minutes. Watch out for stray bones and remove them before serving. You can bake, fry, grill, poach, or steam fish. Barbecued fish is full of flavour.

Use a pair of clean tweezers to remove bones.

crab cakes

ingredients serves 4

2 eggs

2 tablespoons parsley

3 tablespoons mayonnaise

2 teaspoons Dijon-style mustard

1/2 teaspoon Worcestershire sauce

2 cans (170g each) crabmeat, drained

1 cup (100g) dry breadcrumbs

flour for dusting

3 tablespoons (50g) butter

tools to use

whisk, mixing bowl, kitchen knife, cutting board, wooden spoon, can opener, metal spoon, plate, frying pan, metal spatula, oven mitts

For a change of pace, try using a can of tuna fish instead of crabmeat.

1 Whisk the eggs in a mixing bowl. Finely chop the parsley and add it to the bowl along with the mayonnaise, mustard, and Worcestershire sauce. Mix everything together well.

2 Open the cans of crabmeat, being careful to avoid the sharp edges. Spoon the crabmeat onto a plate and check to make sure there are no bits of shell.

3 Add the breadcrumbs and crab meat to the egg mixture. Mix everything together well. Divide the mixture into eight mounds. Dust your hands with flour. Shape each mound into a ball. Place the balls onto a lightly floured cutting board and press down gently to flatten.

4 Melt the butter in a frying pan over low heat. Put the crab cakes gently into the frying pan. Turn the heat up slightly and cook over medium heat for about 4 minutes. When the bottoms of the crab cakes are golden brown, use a metal spatula to turn them over. Cook the other sides for another 4 minutes.

meat and chicken

One of the simplest ways to prepare a delicious meal is to cook meat on a barbecue grill. Serve it sizzling and juicy, straight from the fire. Add a simple salad, rice or potatoes and everyone will go home full. If it rains, use the broiler instead!

Well cooked? Some people prefer beef pink in the center, while others like it well-cooked with a crispy coat. Pork and chicken must always be cooked all the way through.

Buying meat Most people buy packaged meat which has been trimmed of most of its fat and cut into pieces. Allow about 3 – 5 oz. of lean meat for each person. Read the label on the meat package. It will tell you the weight, price, and the kind of "cut" it is.

Store meat in the refrigerator or freezer until you need to use it. Cover it with plastic food wrap.

steak

mincemeat

sausages

bacon

Cooking meat Barbecuing is one way to cook meat, but there are lots of others! Small, lean cuts of meat can be broiled or fried. Large, thick cuts are best roasted or stewed. Always check the recipe for cooking temperatures and times. Herbs, such as rosemary and thyme, go well with most meat.

Getting saucy Sauces and gravy are often served with meat. A favorite is peanut sauce, which is delicious with kebabs. Mix together 6 tablespoons peanut butter, 1 cup (235ml) water, 2 teaspoons brown sugar, 1 teaspoon finely chopped garlic, 2 tablespoons soy sauce, and a little lemon juice. Put in a small saucepan over a low heat and stir until heated through.

chicken kebabs

ingredients serves 4

4 chicken breasts

2 medium-sized onions

1 strip lemon rind

1 tablespoon soy sauce

3 tablespoons oil

2 teaspoons ground coriander

1 teaspoon ground cumin

1 teaspoon cinnamon

1 teaspoon salt

1 teaspoon turmeric

1 tablespoon sugar

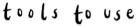

tools to use

kitchen knife, kitchen scissors, cutting board, mixing bowl, grater, electric blender, wooden skewers, oven mitts

Serve the chicken kebabs with a crispy, green salad and rice.

1 Use kitchen scissors or a knife to cut the chicken breasts into 1-inch (3cm) chunks. Put them in a mixing bowl.

2 Now make a paste to flavor the chicken. Chop the onion. Peel a thin strip of lemon rind. Chop it up finely. Put all the ingredients, except the chicken, in a blender. Blend into a paste. Mix the chicken with the paste in a bowl. Cover and put in the refrigerator for at least an hour.

3 Soak the wooden skewers in water to keep them from burning on the grill. Thread the chicken pieces onto the sticks. Lay the kebabs on a hot grill, or under the broiler in the oven. Cook for about 8 minutes. Turn the kebabs over and cook for another 8 minutes. The chicken should be brown and crispy on the outside and thoroughly cooked in the center.

Don't try to put too many pieces onto each stick or the meat won't cook properly.

pastry

If you are thinking of making a tart or a pie, you will need to make some pastry first! There are lots of different kinds of pastry, light and flaky or rich and smooth. All pastry is made from flour, fat such as butter or shortening, and liquid – either water, milk, or egg.

For the best results, use very cold fat, cold water and work in a cool kitchen.

Rubbing in Put the flour and fat into a mixing bowl. Rub the mixture together between your fingertips as lightly as possible. Keep going until the mixture looks like fine breadcrumbs.

Mixing Stir in the liquid, a little at a time. If you add too much liquid, the dough will be too sticky. If you don't add enough liquid, the pastry will be crumbly and hard to roll out.

On a roll Put your pastry on a floured work surface. Sprinkle a little flour on the rolling pin. Roll from the middle outwards. Lift and turn the dough as you work.

savory vegetable quiche

sweet apple tart

Into the pan Line a pie plate with the pastry and smooth out the edges. Fill in any holes with scraps. Moisten the edges of the scraps with cold water and gently press in place. Some recipes tell you to bake the pastry crust halfway before adding the filling. A pie has pastry on top, A tart has pastry only on the bottom.

ingredients

Pastry

1 cup (140g) pastry flour plus extra for working

2 tablespoons (50g) vegetable shortening

2 tablespoons (50g) butter plus extra for greasing

2 – 3 tablespoons water

salt

Filling

1/3 cup (80g) butter

1/3 cup (100g) sugar

1 teaspoon vanilla extract

2 – 3 cooking apples

2 eggs

tools to use

large and small mixing bowls, kitchen knife, cutting board, rolling pin, 7-inch springform pan, plastic kitchen wrap, small saucepan, wooden spoon, vegetable peeler, grater, oven mitts

Choose your filling – sweet and juicy fruits or savory cheese and egg.

1 Heat the oven to 325°F. Make the pastry. Put the flour in the large mixing bowl with the salt. Then cut the shortening and butter into small pieces. Use your fingertips to rub the fats into the flour until the mixture looks like coarse crumbs. Add enough water to make a ball of soft dough.

2 Sprinkle a little flour onto a clean work surface. Use a rolling pin to roll the pastry out to a thickness of about 1/8 inch. Drape the pastry over the rolling pin and lift it over the springform pan. Push the pastry gently into the pan and smooth out the edges with a knife. Cover with plastic kitchen wrap and put the pan in the refrigerator while you make the filling.

3 Now make the filling. Melt the butter in a small saucepan over low heat. Let cool slightly. Add the sugar, vanilla, and eggs. Mix well.

4 Peel the apples. Grate the apples into a mixing bowl. Mix in the butter, sugar, and egg mixture. Pour over the pastry crust. Bake for about 45 minutes, or until the apples and crust are golden brown. Let the tart cool before removing from pan.

cakes and muffins

You don't need a birthday to make a cake. Light and puffy or rich and fruity, there are cakes for every occasion – or no occasion at all! Small rolls and muffins make a delicious morning or afternoon treat.

Heavy or light Cakes with a lot of fruit and fat in them take longer to bake than light sponge cakes containing little or no fat. The fat content means that the cake will keep longer. Sponge cakes with no fat should be eaten the same day.

Testing time Recipes give cooking times, but always test to see if your cake is baked all the way through. With fruit cakes, poke a skewer into the center. If it comes out clean, your cake is done. For sponge cakes, lightly press the surface. If the cake springs back, it is ready.

Out of the pan Taking your cake out of the baking pan can be a bit of a problem! To help, before baking, line the pan with grease-proof paper, or grease it with a little butter or shortening. After baking, let the cake cool. Run the blade of a knife between the cake and the pan. Turn onto a wire rack to cool.

Decorating cakes can be as simple as this. Frost the top of the cake and sprinkle on tiny candies in all the colors of the rainbow!

To stop your cake sinking, leave the oven shut until near the end of cooking time.

chocolate muffins

Chocolate-filled roll

fruit cake

28

honey cake

ingredients

1/3 cup (100ml) honey
1 stick (1/2 cup) butter
1/3 cup (100g) sugar
2 eggs
4 tablespoons water
1 cup (140g) pastry flour
1/2 teaspoon baking powder
1 teaspoon baking soda
pinch of salt
small package of sliced almonds

tools to use

saucepan, mixing bowl to fit neatly
over saucepan, large mixing bowl,
electric beater or whisk,
wooden spoon, metal spoon,
8-inch cake pan, baking tray, oven mitts

Sprinkle the top of the cake with sliced, toasted almonds, or dust with powdered sugar.

1 Heat the oven to 350°F. Put some water in the saucepan. Set the mixing bowl on top. Put the honey and butter in the bowl. Gently heat the water without allowing it to boil. Stir until the honey and butter melt. Turn off the heat.

2 Put the sugar in a mixing bowl and add the eggs. Use an electric beater to beat the mixture until it is pale and creamy. This will take 5 – 10 minutes. You can beat it by hand using a whisk but this is tiring and takes longer.

3 Add the honey and butter mixture to the beaten sugar and egg, a spoonful at a time. Stir between each spoonful. Add the 4 tablespoons of water and stir well.

4 Add the flour, baking powder, baking soda, and salt to the bowl. Use a metal spoon to *fold*, or gently stir, the honey and butter mixture into the flour mixture.

5 Grease the baking pan with a little melted butter. Pour in the cake butter. Bake for about 40 minutes. Test to see if it is ready (see instructions opposite). Take the cake out of the oven. When it is cool, take it out of the pan. As the oven cools down, toast the sliced almonds on a baking tray. Scatter them over the top of the warm cake.

breads and rolls

Freshly baked bread smells delicious, but it's even better when you taste it! Because you need only very basic ingredients – flour and water – bread is the most widely eaten food in the world!

Kneading Dust your hands with flour. Use the palms of your hands to push down hard and away from your body. Fold the dough over towards you and push down again. Turn the dough. Keep going until it is smooth and stretchy.

Raised or flat? Raised breads are sometimes called yeast breads after their magic ingredient. Yeast reacts with other ingredients – usually flour and water – to make dough double in size. Flat breads, made without yeast, include Mexican tortillas, Indian chapattis, and Middle Eastern bread. They are quicker to make.

Brown or white? There are lots of different kinds of flour. Flour affects the color and taste of your bread. Wholewheat or rye flour mixed half and half with white flour makes a delicious golden bread.

Tap the base of a loaf. If it sounds hollow, it is done!

Kneading can take up to 10 minutes. Make sure you feel strong before you start!

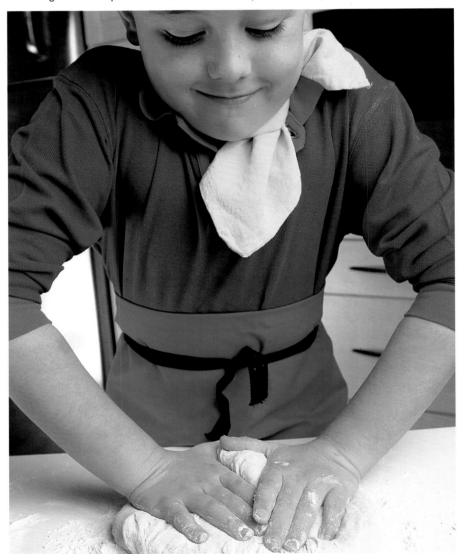

plaits and rolls

ingredients

makes 2 loaves or 12 rolls

2 tablespoons (50ml) very warm (but not
   hot) water

1/4 oz. (7g) packet of dried yeast

1 teaspoon sugar

1 cup (225ml) milk

3 tablespoons (50g) butter

1/2 teaspoon salt

6 cups (990g) all-purpose flour

plus 2 tablespoons flour for kneading

tools to use

1 small and 2 large mixing bowls,
wooden spoon, small saucepan,
damp cloth, baking pan, oven mitts

Serve crispy, home-made rolls with soup and salad, or as a snack with cheese.

1 Put the warm water in a small bowl.
Add the yeast and sugar. Stir well.
Leave the mixture in a warm place for
about 10 minutes. It should start to bubble.

2 Put the milk in a pan over low
heat. Add the butter and salt and
heat until the butter has melted.
Pour the mixture into a large mixing bowl.
Add the bubbling yeast. Add the flour a little
at a time, stirring after each addition. Keep
going until the dough is smooth and elastic,
not too dry and
not too
sticky.

3 Lightly grease the inside of a large
mixing bowl. Put the dough on a
floured surface and start kneading.
(see the instructions opposite). When the
dough is smooth and stretchy, put it in the
bowl. Cover with a damp, clean cloth or
plastic kitchen wrap. Leave in a warm place
for about 1 hour. The dough should double
in size. Turn the oven to 375°F.

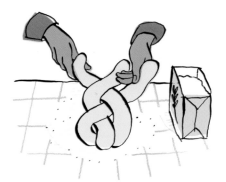

4 Knead the dough again. To make
a braided loaf, start with three
lengths of dough. Braid them
together. Make two loaves the same. Put them
on a floured baking pan. Let stand in a warm
place for about 30 minutes. Put the pan in the
oven. Bake for about 10 minutes. Turn the
heat down to 350°F. Use the chef's tip
opposite to see if the bread is baked through.

index